# HIRING
# HANDBOOK

Easy way of understand "Hiring". A Perfect guide for Starters and Junior Recruiters.

Illustrate by Vijay Anand L.V

# INDEX

# WELCOME HIRING BUDDIES

This book "*Hiring Handbook*" gives you a complete learning experience on the overall recruitment activities on an easy to understand method. The aim of the book is to bridge and convert your theoretical experience into practical experience. It explains the needed basic skills to start your Hiring career and it helps you to be a Successful Recruiter.

It is a first of its kind "*Hiring Handbook*" across the globe and best guide for people who are passionate taking Recruitment as their career. It is a complete package of practical experience which will be useful for Recruiters in both Corporate and Recruitment Agency Environment. It gives you the first hand information on your day to day hiring life and adds value to your hiring.

**This Book guides you on the following topics:**

- Recruitment Lifecycle
- Recruitment Planning
- Market Mapping
- Sourcing Methods
- Screening Methods
- Types and Methods of Interview
- Selection Process
- Offer Process
- Joining or On-Boarding
- Recruitment Policy
- KRA of a Recruiter.
- Practical Hiring.

# HIRING LOBBY

Good to see you in the Recruitment Lobby!!!

Recruitment (Hiring) is a process by which recruiter finds the right talent in the industry on time, for the job opening in his / her / client's company. Recruiter should understand that, recruitment is a job which has to be done with lot of passion and pride.

A Successful Recruiter should posses:

    a.  Good Attitude.

    b.  Good Communication.

    c.  Perseverance.

    d.  Ability to Learn.

    e.  Self Driven.

    f.  Team Oriented.

    g.  Hiring Skills.

    h.  Technical Domain Knowledge.

    i.  Achieve Targets.

    j.  Market Mapping Skills.

    k.  Ability to interact (Candidates / Clients).

    l.  Convincing Skills.

    m.  Offer to Joining Ratio.

Before you go into the details, you should be clear with the common terms referred in the Recruitment Industry.

# COMMON TERMS IN THE RECRUITMENT INDUSTRY

1. **Client** – For Corporate, the term refers to the people who give projects for them.

   – For Recruitment Agency, the term refers to the Corporate HR who gives them assignments.

2. **Candidates** – People who are applying for job. They are also known as Applicants or Resources.

3. **Consultants** – Recruitment / Placement Agency.

4. **Corporate** – Company with all Professional set-ups.

5. **Hiring Manager** – The person who heads the team of recruiters.

6. **Recruiter** – The person who finds the suitable candidates for the company.

7. **Internal or In-house** – This refers to the employees working in the Company or in the Recruitment Agency.

8. **External** – Referred to people who are not working with their Company.

9. **Opening** – Job Availability.

10. **Job Description** – Also known as Job Specs. It is a write up to make the consultants or the candidates understand on the expectation of the company.

11. **Sourcing** – Process of finding candidates.

12. **Selection** – Candidates who has cleared the interview.

13. **Offer** – A letter to authenticate and indicate the selection of the candidate.

14. **On-Boarding** – A process to help new candidates to become an active member of the company.

15. **No Show** – After commitment the candidate does not show up for interview or for joining.

Let us see what are all the important steps involved in "Hiring Process"....

# CABIN 1 – RECRUITMENT POLICY

Each company has their own recruitment policy connected with the company's goal and mission. Before hiring, the recruiter needs to understand and follow the company's Recruitment Policy. Below given are commonly applicable points across the companies.

- Hiring Company knows that their employees are the key fundamental success to achieve their goals and mission.

- The Hiring Company should implement a strategic and ethical process in hiring in order to achieve best of the skills and attributes to fulfill their company's goal.

- The Company's hiring to be done on an ethical manner where there is a systematic, effective, efficient rule is followed with equal amount of opportunity for skilled candidates.

- By appointing highly skilled staffs, the image / growth of the company go high.

- Recruiters should understand that any kind of poor communications about the company and project will affect the image of the company and affect the staff hiring.

- Company supports the Recruitment process framed by the Recruitment Manager. At anytime the Management is available for support and advice.

- Recruitment Manager is responsible to frame a Recruitment Process in order to fulfill the staffing needs of the company.

- Recruitment Manager has authority to decide on the work allocation for his team. Intimation to be given to the Management and when there is a change, the same has to be kept updated.

- Recruitment Manager streamlines the Recruitment Process and is responsible to hire Right Candidate for the Right Job on a Right time.

- Recruitment Manager is responsible to build the best branding of the company's image among the candidates to attract the highly skilled candidate.

- Whenever there is a staffing need from the client, Recruitment Manager is authorized to initiate the recruitment at any point of the time in a year.

- Recruitment Manager is authorized to fulfill all the staffing needs of the company irrespective of Skills, Functions, Levels and hierarchy.

- Recruitment Manager allocates job to his team members and monitors their recruitment activities through Daily MIS, Weekly MIS and a Monthly MIS.

- Recruitment Manager / Recruiter send the Staff Request form to the Offshore Manager, Functional / Technical Heads to fill the job opening and its descriptions.

- On receiving the staff requisition details, Recruiter gets the approval from the Recruitment Manager or Management to initiate the hiring.

- Recruitment Manager checks with the HR Manager in order to see if any internal staffs can be moved for the newly requested job. On availability, the positions are treated as closed and same is intimated to the client. If not, the external hiring process begins.

- Recruiter understands the expectations of the client / offshore manager like Educational Background, Percentage, Skills, and Experience etc. If the candidates are skilled and does not meet any of the other expectation of the client / off shore manager, the deviation has to be approved by the concern member before hiring.

- Recruiter looks for suitable candidates through various Recruitment Methods discussed and approved by the Management. Any changes in the Recruitment Methods need to be discussed with the Management. Only approved methods need to be followed by the recruiter.

- Recruiter's key result area is to attract the right talent for the right job on right time and performance will be measured with the help of recruitment MIS submitted by the Recruiter.

- Recruitment Manager takes decisions on accepting new recruitment agency or to continue with the existing agencies, Job portals, Advertisement etc based on the past hiring experience.

- Interview Assessment Form needs to be filled by the interview panel on completing the interview. Recruiter has to attach the interview assessment form with the updated resume for next level process.

- Recruiter co-ordinates with the Management, seniors, Interview Panel and the Candidates to complete the Recruitment Life Cycle.

- Recruiter is responsible to verify the information mentioned by the candidate in the resume is true, resulting in offer process.

- Recruiter hand holds the candidate after offering and makes him/her to join the company on the committed date.

- Recruiter verifies the candidate's required documents for joining and helps on smooth On-boarding into the project.

# CABIN 2 – RECRUITMENT LIFE CYCLE

Recruitment Life Cycle is the first phase of the recruitment activity and the entire lifecycle includes from job opening from the Client till Candidates joining and closing the position. Recruiter should be hands-on in Recruitment Life Cycle to understand the other Hiring activities.

ILLUSTRATION ON THE RECRUITMENT LIFE CYCLE in a CORPORATE SECTOR:

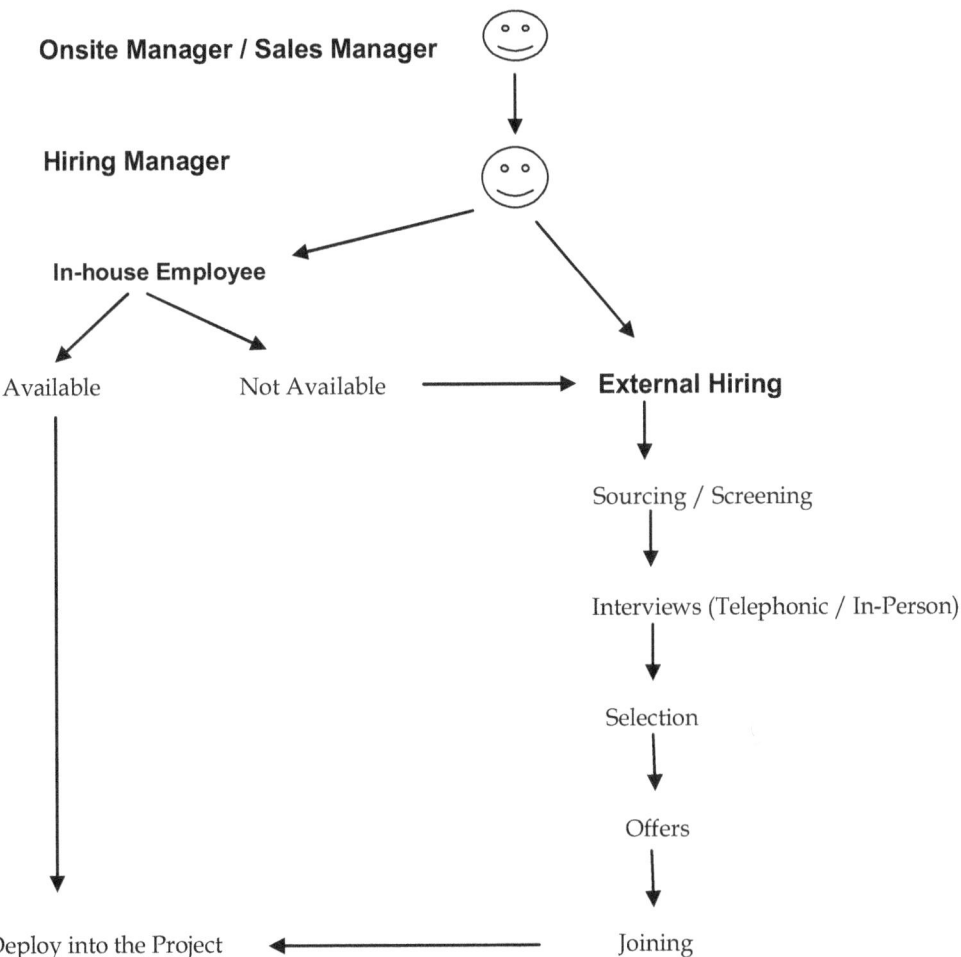

**Gist of the Recruitment Life Cycle:**

- o  Onsite Manager / Project Manager / Sales Manager– Responsible for bringing new opportunities to the Company gets requirement from the client.

- o  Hiring Manager gets the requirement from the Onsite Manager / Project Manager / Sales Manager.

o The Hiring Manager checks with his internal employee database to see if there are any suitable resources available to deploy them into the projects.

o If not, the Hiring Manager gets an approval from the Management to look for suitable candidates from the marketplace.

o In-house Recruiter(s) get the requirement from the Hiring Manager and Market mapping is done by the Recruiters to understand the availability of the candidates.

o Recruiters start to target suitable candidates via various sourcing techniques.

o Interviews are arranged with the Offshore and / or Onsite Manager(s) to find the suitable candidates.

o Selected candidate(s) are offered after HR Interviews.

o Selected Candidate(s) Joins the company and deployed into the projects.

----XXXX-----

In a **RECRUITMENT AGENCY:**

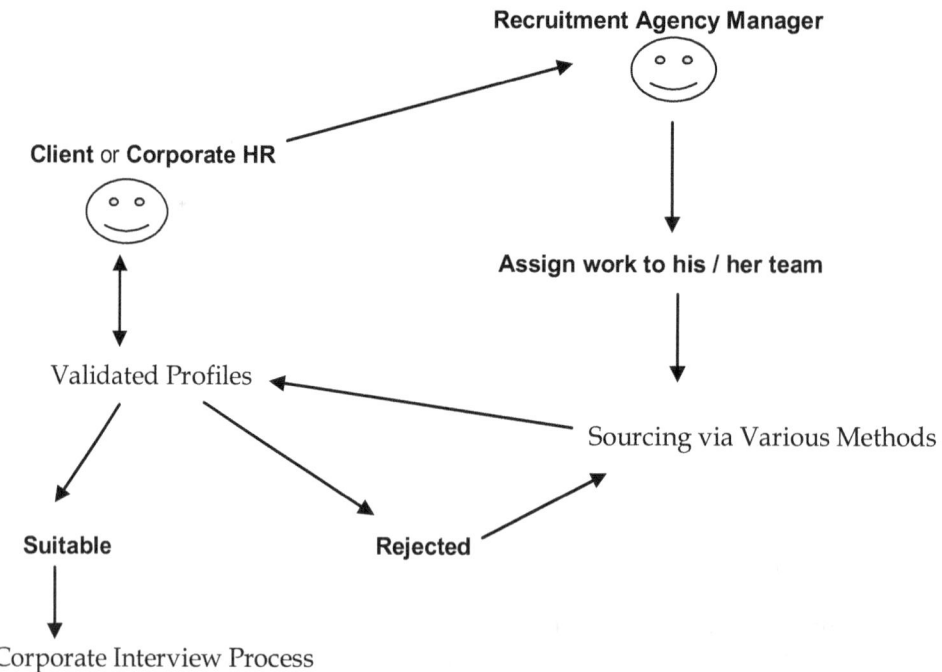

**Gist of the Recruitment Life Cycle:**

- o Here, the Recruitment Agency does not have access to the Onsite Project Managers / Sales Managers.

- o Recruitment Agency works for the requirement received from the Corporate HR.

- o Business Development Manager or the Agency Manager gets the requirement from the Corporate HR.

- o Agency Manager assigns work to their recruiters.

- o Market mapping is done by the Recruiters to understand the availability of the candidates.

- o Recruiter source resumes via various sourcing methods.

- o Validated profiles are sent for the Corporate HR's review.

- o If profiles are not suitable, the Recruiters in Recruitment Agency are advised to look for some more profiles.

- o If the profiles are suitable then the candidates are taken care by the Corporate Recruiters to put them on to the next level of process.

- o Recruiters in the Recruitment Agency hand hold the offered candidates till their joining.

# CABIN 3 – RECRUITMENT PLANNING

Recruitment Planning is a strategy developed by a recruiter before getting into action. It is a plan of hiring activities from Job initiation till closing the position.

The plan includes the following;

a. Position opened date.

b. Number of open positions.

c. Skills needed.

d. Work Location.

e. Maximum Budget.

f. Sourcing Methods.

g. Interview Panel.

h. Interview types.

i. First position to be closed on (date).

j. Maximum days to close the positions.

*For example;*

If there are 5 open positions, as a recruiter you need to draft a revise strategy.

**Open positions**    : 05

**Offers made**      : 10

**Selection**        : 20

**Interviewed**      : 40

**Resume Sourced : 80**

> *Considering 50% as joining and offer accepting ratio, this data has been prepared. The ratio given here is approximate and when you prepare a plan, you can mention a ratio depends upon your experience.*

So the recruiter needs to source an average of 80 resumes to close 5 positions. For every 9 resume sourced, 1 position gets filled on a ratio of 9:1.

The ratio differs from one recruiter to another; a good recruiter is one who reduces ratio of number of profiles sourced and positions closed.

# CABIN 4 – RECRUITMENT CYCLE TIME

Recruitment Cycle Time is defined as no of days taken to close the open positions from the date of initiation. There needs to be a deadline determined by the Hiring Manager and accepted by the recruiter to close the open positions. The Hit Ratio or the Conversion Ratio is very important as it may prolong or shorten the Recruitment Cycle Time.

### *For Example;*

From the Date of Job Opening to Resume Sourced : 5 days

From Resume Sourced / Validated to Resume Shortlisted : 2 days

From Resume Shortlisted to Interview Scheduled : 2 days

From Resume Interview Scheduled to Candidates Selected : 2 days

From Candidates Selected to Candidates Offered : 2 days

From Candidates Offered to Candidates Joined : 30 days

The above example gives us a Recruitment Cycle Time as 43 days to close a position from the date of job initiation. Depending upon the Recruiter's capacity the cycle time may go high or come down.

# CABIN 5 – MARKET MAPPING

Market Mappings are done to understand / asses / analyze the markets prior to the launch or expansion of the projects in an organization. The outcome report suggests the Recruiter to enable and review the operations and opportunities in the market.

Some of the parameters we need to consider for doing the Market Mapping:

a. The need of the company (Requirements).

b. Open Positions.

c. Time required closing the position (Market availability or the notice period of the candidate).

d. Real availability of the resource in the market.

e. Location availability (volumes in local and out station).

f. Company CTC limitations and Market expectations.

g. Available companies (ex. Tier 1 / 2, Consulting, Mid-size, Startups).

Recruiters have to develop a clear picture on the market status and same should be sent to the hiring manager or the management for review.

The report should also contain:

a. How to meet the target (Requirements).

b. Time needed to close the position.

c. CTC approval (if needed to compete with the market standards).

d. Channels of sourcing.

e. Interview Methods.

f. Plans to travel out stations for recruiting (Optional) etc.

Discuss about the Recruitment Plan and Market mapping with your Hiring Manager or the Management. Once you get an approval then move into the Hiring activities.

# CABIN 6 – SOURCING METHODS

Recruiter(s) goal is to fulfill the given assignment with the suitable candidate(s) on time. Let us discuss the various Sourcing Methods by which Recruiter(s) can target relevant resources.

*FOR **FRESHERS:***

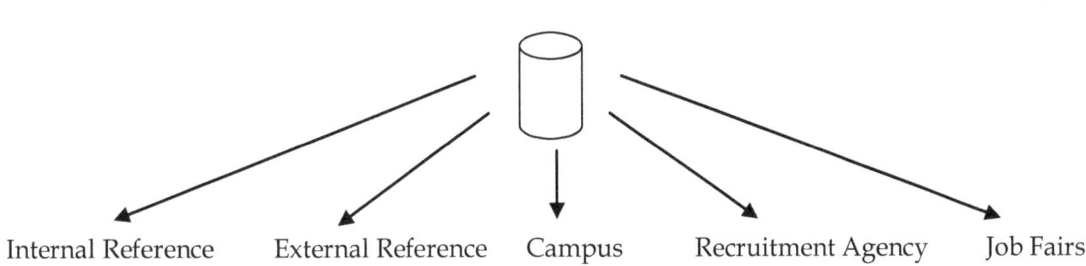

- *Above picture shows the fresher sourcing by the recruiters in corporate environment.*
- *Recruiters in Placement Agency targets fresher from colleges and candidates who apply for their job ad alone.*

### Method 1 - INTERNAL REFERENCE

Most of the companies use Internal Reference as a strategy to motivate the In-house employees by considering the candidates referred by them. It falls under the off campus method.

***Thumbs Up***:
- o Even though internal referrer will not get referral bonus for fresher, he will feel satisfactory by seeing his/her friend gets a job in his company.
- o Number of reference for fresher is high compared to the experienced candidates.

***Thumbs Down***:
- o Too many resumes to filter.
- o Low Academics.
- o Skills and attitude may differ from the job expectation.

### Method 2 - EXTERNAL REFERENCE

External reference includes employee's friends / relatives and the recruiter's network.

***Thumbs Up***: Number of reference for fresher is high compared to the experienced candidates.

***Thumbs Down***:
- o External referred will not get any monetary benefit. So interest to refer will be less.
- o Year of passing and academics.
- o Irrelevant skills.

## Method 3 – CAMPUS

It is a Primary source for recruiters to hire fresher. Most of the Tier1 / 2 companies hire only the core students with high academics and strong communication / analytical skills.

*Thumbs Up*:
- o The recruiter is clear about the educational institution and the breed of candidates available for hiring.
- o Complete support from the Institute Placement Officer.
- o Information on the company is intimated to the students.

*Thumbs Down*:
- o Too many competitors to reserve the highly skilled students.
- o If you are late, you only get students with low academics.
- o All the students expect to be placed in Tier 1 / 2 companies.
- o Comparison of salary with the students placed in familiar companies.

## Method 4 - RECRUITMENT AGENCY (FOR FRESHERS)

There are few recruitment agencies which concentrate only on fresher placements. Since the Tier 1 / 2 companies hire the core candidates from the colleges, the rest of the companies are left with students to be placed. The placement agency forms a bridge between colleges and the corporate to fulfill their fresher needs.

*Thumbs Up*:
- o Recruiters get good candidates from out stations or from other states.
- o Co-ordination from the institution and the recruitment agency.

*Thumbs Down*:
- o Not many companies are interested to hire fresher through the recruitment agency even though there is no billing.
- o Technical Panel availability to travel out station.

## Method 4 – JOB FAIRS

Job fairs are conducted either by the Company or by the third parties like NGO, Job Portal, Employment News Print, Sponsorship Companies etc; this is one kind of the platform for the fresher to meet Companies and find a job. Job fairs are always planned and focused mostly for fresher. Experienced professionals do not prefer to participate in Job Fairs and mostly expects to meet the client in their Office.

*Thumbs Up*:
- o One place where a fresher can meet multiple companies.
- o Companies has an option to meet the out station candidates.
- o Popularizing the brand name of the company by participating or promoting the Job fair.
- o Too many participants.

***Thumbs Down***:
- o Since there are too many applicants, only brief face to face is possible for the HR.
- o Less time spent with the participants.
- o No possibility of written tests.

----xxxx-----

*FOR* **LATERALS TO MID LEVEL EXPERIENCE:**

The strategy to source laterals and mid level experience candidates are different than the entry level applicants.

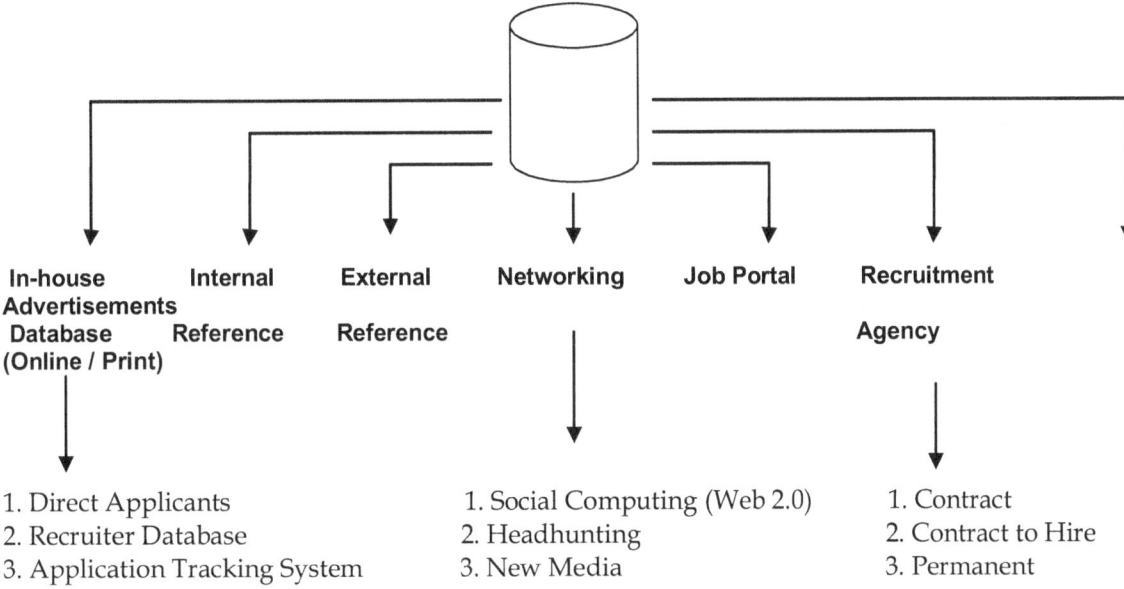

| In-house | Internal | External | Networking | Job Portal | Recruitment |
| Advertisements | | | | | |
| Database | Reference | Reference | | | Agency |
| (Online / Print) | | | | | |

| | | | | | |
|---|---|---|---|---|---|
| 1. Direct Applicants | | 1. Social Computing (Web 2.0) | | 1. Contract | |
| 2. Recruiter Database | | 2. Headhunting | | 2. Contract to Hire | |
| 3. Application Tracking System | | 3. New Media | | 3. Permanent | |

> ➤ *Above picture illustrates the sourcing methods of Corporate Recruiters.*
> ➤ *Recruiters in the Placement Agency may have an internal database, but there is no Internal Reference and an agency for them to support.*

Let us see in detail on the above mentioned sourcing methods;

**Method 1 - IN-HOUSE DATABASE**

### 1. Direct Applicants

One of the old method of getting resumes from the candidates. Before internet era, candidates used to submit their resumes via post and in person.

Once the Internet became common and popular, candidates started submitting their resumes via company website. The resumes can be saved in the recruiter's database.

***Thumbs Up***:
- o It shows the commitment and interest level of the candidate on applying the job in person.
- o Candidates cannot goof up with their profile and identity.

***Thumbs Down***:
- o The growth of the electronic medium has zeroed the effort of the candidates applying the job in person.
- o Nil knowledge / strategy of the candidates to approach the company in-person.

## 2. Recruiter Database

Each recruiter has to build his/her own resume database in order to screen and reserve the resume for future openings. Earlier days the recruiters received the resumes as hard copy. The resumes were stored in a file according to their experience and skills. Every time when there is a job opening, recruiters used to open the file to find the suitable resumes for their opening.

Now a day, with the help of electronic medium recruiters can save the softcopy of the resume on their own database. The resumes can be stored according to their skills and experience. They can update the availability of the candidates from time to time. This should be the first step for the recruiters to search for the candidates before going to the marketplace.

***Thumbs Up***:
- o When there is an opening, it gives immediate access to the recruiters to search for the candidates.
- o Before going into other sourcing methods, recruiter has to make sure if he has the suitable resume in his own database.

***Thumbs Down***:
- o The access is reduced to single person.
- o Not sure if the candidates will be available (if the resume was sent some time back).
- o The skills and experience may vary from time to time. Not all the time the resumes in the recruiter database will suit the opening.

## 3. Application Tracking System (Recruitment Software)

- o It is an Electronic way of approaching the hiring process. The software gives the access to centralized database for all the recruiters.
- o It acts as an assistant for the recruiters and gives all the information such as Candidate Name, Location, Skills, Experience, if the they have appeared before, interview date etc.,
- o It helps the candidate to track the candidate's record without many efforts.
- o The software controls the recruitment life cycle and it follows all the steps from Candidate's filtering to on-boarding.

- The software automatically sends the recruitment or job opening information to the candidate.
- It is available in Product and SAAS model.
- Product type of Recruitment Software can be used inside the organization alone. But in SaaS model, you can access the application where ever you get an internet connection.

*Thumbs Up*:
- The software controls all the activities of the recruitment and helps recruiters on each step.
- Filtering, screening and finding the track of candidate's history is very easy.
- Access to multiple recruiters.
- Regular newsletter to the candidate to update their resume for future openings, new job openings and reference.

*Thumbs Down*:
- Products are Costly – Not affordable for small to mid size company.
- Complex system – Needs to do lot of data input of the candidate to get a result.
- It depends on other sourcing methods.

## *Method 2 - INTERNAL OR EMPLOYEE REFERENCE*

Every employee has to know the new openings, updates or the closure of the previous openings has to be communicated on a regular interval. Not only for referring candidates but also as a policy there has to be a clear communication between HR and employees.

There are few things to be considered for internal reference.
- The longevity of the referred candidate staying with the company is high.
- Chances of getting good profiles which is not available in Job Portal or any other sourcing methods.
- Referred employee gets referral bonus and thus the percentage of reference goes high.

Few ways of communication are;

### *1. Direct internal email (Bulk Email Blast)*

An email blast to all the employees will communicate the needed updates with least effort. The name and email id of the Recruiter has to be mentioned in the email so that the referred resumes reached the concern HR.

### *2. Notice Board Display*

A gist of the job opening in the office notice board will create a buzz among the employees. It will make employees to see repeatedly when they pass by the notice board.

*Thumbs Up*:
- Strong employee reference can bring new profiles.

- o Passive job seekers may turn as an active job seeker by passing on the information of the project like Skills  Career growth, Salary etc.,
- o Referral amount as a motivation apart from Salary.

### Thumbs Down:
- o Chances of getting more junk profiles and it may eat more time of the recruiters on filtering the resume.
- o Duplicate profile – Recruiter might have received the same resume referred by the employee.
- o Sometimes referral amount may not create interest among the employees.
- o Chances of some employees not receiving the email blast due to various reasons.
- o Too many notices or improper placement of the job opening in the notice board deviate the employee's concentration.

## Method 3 - EXTERNAL REFERENCE

External reference includes employee's friends / relatives and the recruiter's network.

### Thumbs Up:
- o Resumes which are not available in the job portal.
- o Applicant's trust on his/her referrer and longevity of staying with the company.

### Thumbs Down:
- o External referred will not get any monetary benefit. So interest to refer will be less.
- o Irrelevant skills.
- o Time to filter the profiles.

## Method 4 - NETWORKING

### 1. Head Hunting

Head Hunting is a recruitment process by which the recruiter finds the candidates in Non-traditional way. When all the channels like Internal and external reference, Job portal & database are dried with viewed profiles, the next step of the recruiter is to hunt for passive talents in the Industry. A head hunter has to be very strong sourcing and convincing skills. Majority of the head hunters are with the recruitment agency and few in corporate. Before head hunting, the recruiter needs to check with corporate and get reference if there are any competitors in the market who works on the same kind of domain / projects.

*What will happen if all the sourcing channels are closed for recruiters?*

Real head hunter reads the entire resume he gets and keeps in memory, which company works on what technology. Head hunter calls the company and randomly spills some name to the receptionist to connect into a specified project. He / She then talks to the unknown person to check if the candidate has a relatively potential skills in-line to his expectation.

If the candidate is interested and suitable, the interview process continues.
If the candidate is not interested, headhunter gets reference from the unknown candidate.

*Thumbs Up*:
- o Sometimes, clients provide reference of the available candidates who are suitable for their projects.
- o Chances of getting suitable resumes are high.
- o Passive job seeker gets active.

*Thumbs Down*:
- o Candidates have to be reached through company board number.
- o Unwanted questions and check from Receptionist / other members.
- o Candidates get irritated by the anonymous person.
- o Fear of internal tracing.

## 2. Social Computing (Web 2.0 Methods)

Off late, there is enormous growth in the internet. The new way of attracting talent is by social computing like Twitter, Facebook, Linkedin etc, social computing has become common to all and the engagement of friends / unknown talents has become simple. Recruiter targets individuals or a group by spreading the current job openings available in his / her company. People who are interested for the job reciprocate to the recruiter and others pass it on to their network of people. Headhunting has become so simple in the electronic format. Recruiters write blogs and post his comments in open forums to make sure they indirectly create the interest in the candidate to apply for job.

*Thumbs Up*:
- o Connect individuals and Group with a request.
- o Tap candidates based on the location and skills.
- o Candidate's background, credentials, recommendations are available open.
- o Viral sharing of the job opening.
- o Quick turnaround time of sourcing.

*Thumbs Down*:
- o Most of them connect only with limited members.
- o Danger of blocking the recruiters for spamming.

## 3. New Media

New Media is a modern way of hiring resources. It includes Video Conferencing, Webcasting and any hiring happens through media. This method of hiring is popular in western countries and it is picking up in other countries too.

Candidates now have lot of options to look out, so time taken to contact / interview them may provide advantage for other recruiters. Immediate engagement of the available resources is important. New media helps recruiters to contact available resources where ever they are. When the job opening is published in the job portal / social computing or an email sent to the candidate, recruiter attaches his new media link. Interested candidates approach the candidate immediately, so that the recruiter can do basic level screening to find the suitability of the resource.

Candidates who are in same location seldom get time to appear for interview in person. Mostly when the candidate is available after his / her office hour, recruiters and the technical panels are not available. New Media bridges the gap between the candidate and the corporate, enables / connects them immediately.

### *Thumbs Up*:
- o Instant reach of the candidate.
- o Anytime Interview.
- o By seeing the person virtually candidate's identification are stored and malpractice is avoided.
- o Option of recording the interview for future reference.

### *Thumbs Down*:
- o Popular only in few countries.
- o Strategy to target.
- o Low awareness of technology among recruiters.

## *Method 5 – JOB PORTAL*

Job Portal is a popular method for sourcing resumes and it acts as a platform for both candidates and the corporate to connect each other.

For job seekers, it is a classifieds of job available in one place. Job seeker creates a profile with all the required information such as name, location, career objective, experience, skills, projects, certifications etc,   They can review the job opening posted by the recruiters and if interested they directly apply with their profile uploaded in the portal.

For recruiters, it acts as an external database of available resources in the market. Recruiters can search the entire database with the relevant keywords such as skills, experience, location; projects etc, if the resumes are suitable, recruiters directly call / email candidates to check their interest.

### *Thumbs Up*:
- o Recruiters and job seekers can access from anywhere. (Cloud Computing Model).
- o Direct access to each other.
- o Simple user interface.
- o Job seeker can create their profile and can upload, edit, save information anytime.

### *Thumbs Down*:
- o Cost of the service.
- o Same profiles across all the job portals.
- o No value added service.
- o High volume of inactive profiles.
- o Recruiter's competency and awareness about the model.

## *Method 6 – RECRUITMENT AGENCY*

The Recruitment Agency is also known as Manpower Agency or a Placement Agency. They act as an external arm of corporate to fulfill their recruitment needs. There are several reasons for engaging Recruitment Agency in Corporate Hiring;
- o  Non availability of Recruiters in Corporate.
- o  Additional support in bulk hiring.
- o  Quick turnaround time of resume.
- o  Get new resumes which are not available in portal.
- o  Head Hunting.
- o  For proper Screening, Validation, Scheduling, On-boarding.

Corporate Recruiter assigns job to the Recruitment Agency in order to get a value addition in hiring. The job of a Recruiter in a Placement Agency has to step into the shoes of the corporate and create interest in the job opening.

### *Merits of a Recruitment Agency:*
- o  Start working on the requirement once assigned.
- o  Resume flow.
- o  Support on bulk and campus hiring.
- o  Support on walk-in interviews (weekday or weekend).
- o  Quick turnaround time for screening / interviews / offers.

### *Improvements needed in a Recruitment Agency:*
- o  Frequent meetings with the Client needed are not happening.
- o  To be spent more time with the Client after office hours.
- o  Understand the real requirement and focus on the same.
- o  Mentoring junior recruiters is required.
- o  Convincing skills.

### *What does a client expects from a Placement Agency?*
- o  Understand the job description thoroughly.
- o  Screen resumes in a proper manner.
- o  Convey proper information to the candidate and make sure he reads the job description.
- o  Quick turnaround of resumes.
- o  Only qualified resumes are sent for client review.
- o  Support on Interview process.
- o  Hand holding of the candidate till joining.

### *What does a Placement agency expects from a Client?*
- o  Clear Job Description.
- o  Real requirements to work.
- o  Time allocate to meet / call for various clarifications.
- o  Quick response on the email / resume sent.
- o  Feedback / intimation on the interviews and offers.
- o  Support to release the placement fee from the finance team.

There are three types of Hiring where a placement agency helps the corporate to identify candidates.

## 1. Contract Staffing

Recruitments are done based on the project duration and skills. The need of the resource may start from few weeks to months and if the candidate cannot be deployed into other projects, corporate go for Contract Staffing or Temporary Hiring. The billing of the resource for limited will be high and corporate pays the recruitment agency every month as a contract pay. Resources will be on the pay roles of the recruitment agency and they pay the monthly salary till the contract gets over.

In Contract staffing the candidate are asked to move out of the pay rolls of the placement agency. There is no commitment that the client will hire the contract employee. Nor there is a guarantee that consultancy will keep them on their payrolls to deploy with some other client opportunity.

***Thumbs Up***:
- o   Immediate resource for corporate and billing for placement agency.

***Thumbs Down***:
- o   Less interest of the candidates for contract.
- o   Profiles availability.
- o   Less jobs for candidates after contract period.
- o   Too many consultants contact same candidates for the same job opening.
- o   Candidates confirm all the consultants to process the resumes.
- o   Habit of not reading the job description from the candidate.
- o   Last minute drop outs (no shows).
- o   Candidate leaves the job in between.

## 2. Contract to Hire

Contract to Hire differs from Contract Staffing. Here there is a commitment from the employer that the resource will be obtained on the pay rolls of the company. Again it is based on the performance of the candidate.

***Thumbs Up***:
- o   Commitment from the employer on direct hire.
- o   Immediate resource for corporate and billing for placement agency.

***Thumbs Down***:
- o   Candidates working in Niche skills aren't interested.
- o   Profiles availability in Market.
- o   Too many consultants contact same candidates for the same job opening.
- o   Candidates confirm all the consultants to process the resumes.
- o   Habit of not reading the job description from the candidate.
- o   Last minute drop outs (no shows).
- o   Candidate leaves the job in between.

## 3. Permanent Hiring

If the contract or contracts to hire candidates leave the job in between, consultants lose billing from that month. Also the credibility of the placement agency comes down. To avoid the difficulty most of the consultants work on Permanent Hiring as there is low risk involved in placing the candidates. Once the requirement is shared, placement agency finds the candidate and processes them with the client. If the candidate joins, they get a onetime percentage (differs from one agency to another) from the company. If the placed candidate leaves the company within 90 days of joining, agency has to refund the amount or place another candidate without any billing.

**Thumbs Up**:
- o   Interest level of the candidates.
- o   Profiles Availability for permanent positions.
- o   Quick turnaround time for processing etc.

**Thumbs Down**:
- o   Candidates get more calls from various consultants for same opening.
- o   Candidates confirm all the consultants to process the resumes.
- o   Habit of not reading the job description from the candidate.
- o   Last minute drop outs (no shows) for interviews / joining.

### Method 7 – ADVERTISEMENTS

### 1. Online

The term "Online" refers to Internet medium which is the most popular and powerful medium. The growth on the internet has ensured the connections of the world wide professionals in a single space. Online ads can be frequently seen where ever there is abundance of resources available.
*Example*
- a.   Job Portal.
- b.   Forums.
- c.   Groups.
- d.   Social Computing Websites.
- e.   Blogs
- f.   PPC / PPV methods.

Candidates who are interested for the job opening can directly apply for the job.
**Thumbs Up**:
- o   Reaches the target audience.
- o   Popularizing the company's brand name in web.
- o   Direct application from the candidate.
- o   Cost effective.
- o   Online Ads can be viewed anywhere in the world.
- o   Ads can be directed to friends by sharing in the web or by an email.

**Thumbs Down**:
- o   We may not know who are interested in a job change.
- o   Work location interest.

## 2. Print

Print Ads are traditional method of approaching the candidates. The growth of internet has reduced the readers and still it has its own growth in the industry. There are few magazines and news papers available in the market which has a special column and supplementary papers for the Job Vacancies. Candidates get to know the details of the vacancy, walk-ins through the news papers.

### Thumbs Up:
- Targets from fresher to senior professionals.
- Direct application from the candidate.

### Thumbs Down:
- Cost of a single ad in a news paper for a week is equal to the cost of the online ad for a month.
- Online has reduced the Print readers.
- Targets a particular editorial region.

# CABIN 7 – SCREENING METHODS

The next step after sourcing is to check the suitability of the resume with the current job openings. The recruiter should check the following in resume before speaking:

- Name, Address, Email id and a contact number.
- Objective.
- Educational Credentials.
- Work Experience.
- Project Summary with project name, client details, location, description, skills, roles and the responsibilities of the candidate.
- Good resume format.

### *How to screen a resume?*

- Before screening a resume, the hiring manager and the recruiters should be clear on the job description, skill knowledge, availability, domain etc.

- It is advisable for hiring manager to have a discussion with the onsite manager / offshore project manager on the skills expectation of the resource.

- It is advisable for recruiters to get enough knowledge on the technical terms mentioned in the job description. Google the web and also discuss with the senior recruiters who has handled similar skills in the past.

- Check for skills mentioned in the resume. If it is not suitable with the job description, drop the resume.

- Check for Educational details to see if the institution, group, percentage, pass-out year are in-line with the Company's policy.

- Check if the current / past working company is not black listed.

- Check for the projects; most importantly the recruiter has to read the project to understand if it has been goofed-up or a genuine.

- Check if the project duration doesn't over laps the other project duration. If yes, ask for explanation from the candidate.

- Check if the required skills for the company are placed properly in the projects. If not, drop the resume.

- The roles and responsibilities mentioned properly and it is in-line with the job description.

- o Do not consider a resume, if the skills of the candidate are mentioned long time back in his/her projects.

- o Check for the candidate's current location. If suitable process for next level. Otherwise check with the hiring manager or management if out station candidates can be considered and then process on the approval.

### *How to screen over phone?*

Phone etiquette acts as one of the important business tool which every recruiter has to posses. Unfortunately, there is lack of knowledge on the subject. A Recruiter is a brand ambassador for the company so; knowing all the etiquettes before calling a person is important.

- o Greet the candidates depending upon the time you call them.

- o Introduce yourself and name of the company you are working for.

- o Check if he/she is busy to discuss on the purpose of the call. If a good time, start explaining about the opening. If not, get a suitable time to discuss.

- o While discussing, put good things about the company, projects, location, turn over, employee strength, previous records etc,

- o Explain the need of skills in the project and duration of the project. Show confidence in your speech to convey a positive message to the candidate.

- o Explain the candidates if it is a long term or short term assignment.

- o Check with the candidate if he/she has appeared for interviews earlier.

- o Check with indirect questions like current project name, client name, duration, team size etc., if the candidate tells the same as mentioned in the resume.

- o Check the interest of the candidates on work location. Some of the local candidates might be looking for out station and some out station candidates might be looking for your job location.

- o Strongly ask for the reason for looking out new options. If it is convincing then process further. If not, drop the candidate.

- o Check doubly with the candidate if the resume gets shortlisted internally, then he/she has to take the interview without fail.

- o Never process candidates if you feel the candidate is not open / not co-operating / bluffing.

- o Check if the Current CTC, Expected CTC and Notice period are in-line with the company policy. If suitable process, if not drop.

- ○ Periodically keep hiring manager informed on the Market Pay.

- ○ Send a detailed job description to the candidate.

- ○ Check if the candidate has gone through the job description properly and understood the suitability.

- ○ Process for interview only if the candidate and you feel fine with the screening process.

# CABIN 8 – TYPES OF INTERVIEW

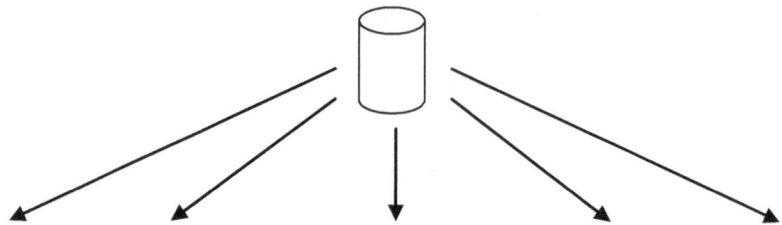

Telephonic Interview    In-Person Interview    Walk-in Interview    Job Fairs    Video Conference

> ➢ *Above picture shows us the various types of interview for the job applicants in the Corporate Environment.*
> ➢ *Recruiters in Recruitment Agency do an initial level screening over phone and supports / arranges the Walk-in, in-person interviews, Job fairs and Video Conference for Corporate.*

### 1. Telephonic Interview

Telephonic interview has become an important interview process in most of the companies. It is widely accepted across the globe as candidates find difficult to attend the interview on a weekday. It avoids people travelling from out station to take their interview. It reduces the traveling charges of the company to be reimbursed for the out station candidates. Also it helps to connect candidates with the onsite manager or the client to assess the candidate's technical ability.

### Thumbs Up:
- o  Avoids the time consumed for travel.
- o  Reduces the Travel cost of the candidate.
- o  Filters junk candidate in the first level screening.
- o  Anytime Interview is possible.
- o  Candidates can be from local or out stations to take the interview.

### Thumbs Down:
- o  Mal practicing over phone is possible. Don't know if the same candidate who has applied is taking the interview.
- o  Attitude of the candidate can't be found.

### 2. In-person Interview

Telephonic interview helps Recruiters to avoid time wasted on junk candidate. But once they found well, there has to be a second level in-person interview to make sure that the candidate who took the telephonic interview is appearing for the second level. In-person interview helps Recruiters to assess candidate's attitude and interest towards the open position. For fresher there has to be an attitude and aptitude test conducted before in-person interview.

In-person interview can be either Technical or HR.

***Thumbs Up***:
- o   Avoids manipulation.
- o   Helps to assess the candidate's attitude and technical skills.

***Thumbs Down***:
- o   Availability of the candidate and the technical panel at a specified time.
- o   Travel constraints for out station candidates.
- o   Expenses for the company to reimburse the travel amount.

### 3. Walk-in Interview

Walk-ins are always planned and mostly organized by the company. It can't be conducted over phone instead all the candidates have to be assembled in one campus to take the interview. Walk-ins are conducted mostly over weekends to help candidates travel from out stations and take the interview comfortably. The Recruiters in Corporate and Recruitment Agency can work together to pull more candidates for the interview.

There has to be a proper plan and following needs to be done for a walk-in;

a.   Filter resumes based on the job description.

b.   Optional of doing a telephonic interview before calling candidates for a walk-in. To avoid junk candidates wasting time in the interview.

c.   Venue needs to be confirmed in advance (Company campus or a Common venue).

d.   Intimate in the venue details and materials required to bring at the time of the interview.

e.   Check with the recruitment agency if the above mentioned details are passed to their candidates.

f.   Follow up and make sure that the technical panels are present on the day to take interviews.

g.   Have couple of interviewers as a back-up (who resides nearby and can come in a short intimation) if the committed interviewer fails to present.

h.   Collect resumes from the candidates who are waiting in the venue and prioritize their interview time based on their arrival.

i.   Facilitate the interview halls with white papers, pen or board with marker, so that it helps candidates to write problems / answers and explain the interviewers about their skills.

j.   Always have an interview feedback form and get the feedback of the interviewer(s) once completing the interview.

k.   Check if the details in the feedback forms are duly filled and signed by the interviewer(s).

l.  Create a report (excel sheet) with number of candidates appeared, cleared and rejected in walk-in.

m.  Send it to the hiring manager / management and keep them intimated on your efforts.

n.  Recruiters in recruitment agency have to remind candidates on the previous day of the walk-in so that they don't forget.

o.  Follow-up over phone or available in-person in the venue to see if the scheduled candidates have come for the interview.

p.  It will be a value addition service to the corporate and will create a good impression on the recruitment agency.

q.  Keep the agency hiring manager intimated on the number of candidates shown for the walk-in, no shows, cleared and rejected.

r.  Send a detailed report to the corporate HR and request for a feedback.

**Thumbs Up**:
- o Only filtered candidates are called for the walk-in.
- o Helps candidates to take interviews on his/her holiday.

**Thumbs Down**:
- o HR interviews should also be done on the same day. Calling the shortlisted candidates on the other day will lose focus and drag the process for some more time.
- o Candidates should not be kept waiting for long time.

### 4. Job Fairs

From a recruiter's point of view, following are the check list to be prepared for a Job Fair:

a.  Candidate's experience level.

b.  Skills.

c.  Number of interviewers needed.

d.  Number of candidates expected.

e.  Coordinate with the administration team to organize the travel.

f.  Facility needed in the venue (for Recruiters / Interviewers).

**Thumbs Up**:
- o One place where a fresher can meet multiple companies.
- o Companies has an option to meet the out station candidates.
- o Popularizing the brand name of the company by participating or promoting the Job fair.
- o Too many participants.

***Thumbs Down***:
- o Since there are too many applicants, only brief face to face is possible for the Technical /HR interviews.
- o Less time spent with the participants.
- o No possibility of written tests.


### 5. Video Conference

Interviewing candidates through Video Conference is one of the modern ways of hiring resources. This method of hiring is popular in western countries and it is picking up in other countries too.

Candidates now have lot of options to look out, so time taken to contact / interview them may provide advantage for other recruiters. Immediate engagement of the available resources is important. New media helps recruiters to contact available resources where ever they are. When the job opening is published in the job portal / social computing or an email sent to the candidate, recruiter attaches his new media link. Interested candidates approach the candidate immediately, so that the recruiter can do basic level screening to find the suitability of the resource.

Candidates who are in same location seldom get time to appear for interview in person. Mostly when the candidate is available after his / her office hour, recruiters and the technical panels are not available. New Media bridges the gap between the candidate and the corporate, enables / connects them immediately.

***Thumbs Up***:
- o Instant reach of the candidate.
- o Anytime Interview.
- o By seeing the person virtually candidate's identification are stored and malpractice is avoided.
- o Option of recording the interview for future reference.

***Thumbs Down***:
- o Popular only in few countries.
- o Strategy to target.
- o Low awareness of technology among recruiters.

# CABIN 9 – INTERVIEW PROCESS

For **CORPORATE ENVIRONMENT:**

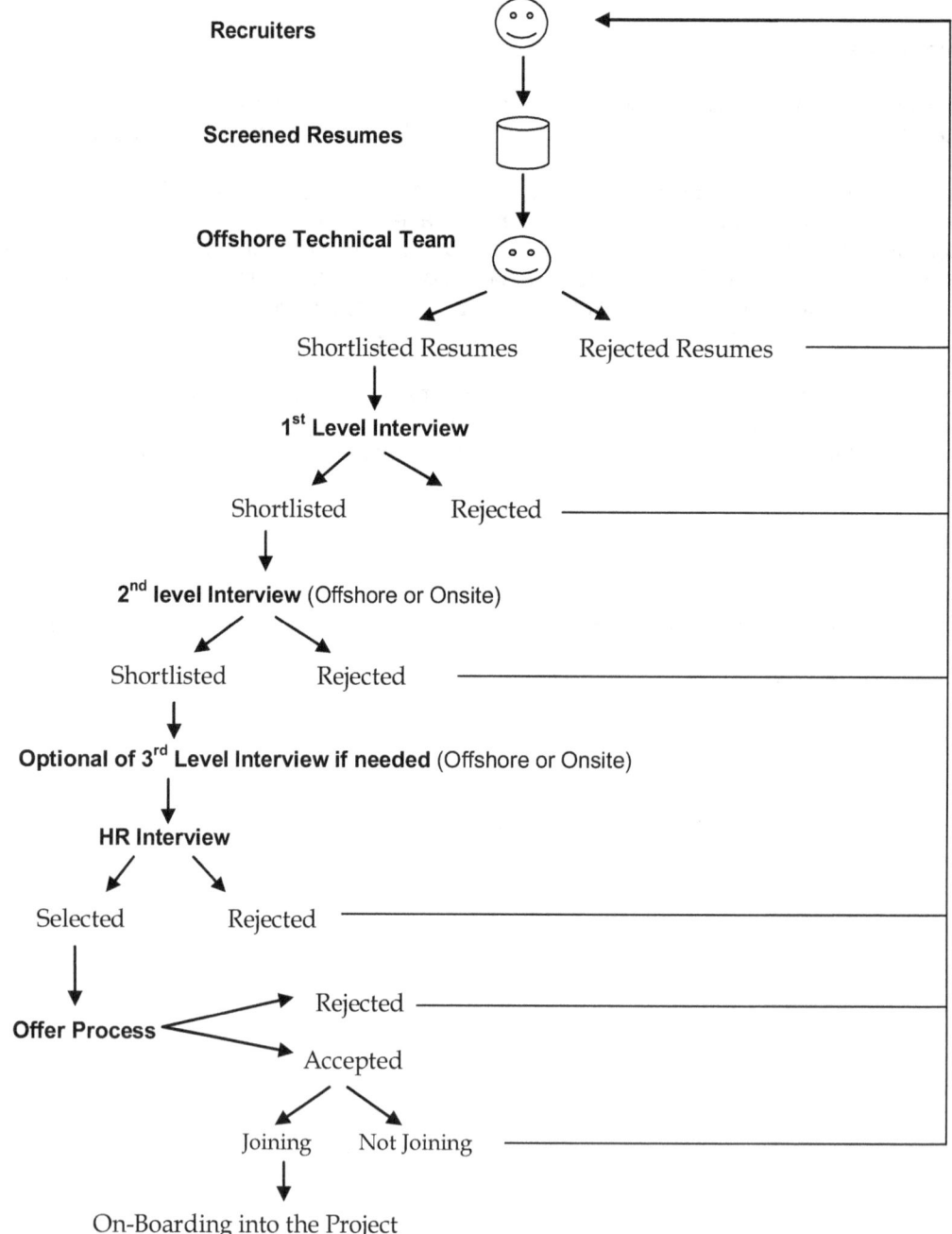

The Recruiter is ready now with the knowledge of Recruitment Life Cycle, Recruitment Planning, Market Mapping, Sourcing and Screening Methods. The next step is to find the potential interview panel that is responsible to take the interviews. Recruiter has to find the availability of both the Candidates as well as the Interview panel members. The panel members should be either from the technical team of the same project the recruiter is going to hire or with the needed skills and understanding of what is required from the candidate which suits the project requirement.

The reason behind why a recruiter has to do a Market Mapping before sourcing / interviewing them is to make a presentation to his/her management on the availability of the resources in the market. Recruiter can't get 100% suitable resumes from the market and the interview panel members can't get 100% suitable skills according to their project expectation. Recruiter should be transparent with the higher officials and the interview crew on the availability of the resources. So on understanding and accepting the market reality both the recruiter and the interviewer has to proceed.

The interview panel not only changes the life of the candidate but also the life of a recruiter. If a recruiter has an understandable interview panel with the common goal to identify a skilled candidate, then the job opening might get closed soon. If a recruiter gets an interview panel that does not stop even after finding a suitable candidate but also to see more and more candidates, then the duration of open positions are high.


### *Process Description:*

Recruiter sends the screened profiles to the Technical Panel. The profiles are reviewed by the technical team in order to see if the profiles are sourced and screened properly in line with the job description. If the resumes are not suitable, the technical team comments and advices recruiter on skills / project / other requirements. For suitable resumes, the technical team asks the recruiter to schedule an interview on their available schedule.

Recruiter then finds the availability of both the technical team and the candidate for a discussion. For out station candidates the interviews can be organized via phone and for local candidates if they cannot appear in person on a weekday, the telephonic interview can be organized.

Recruiter can use any of the interview methods to take the initial level interview with the technical panel. If the candidate performs low in the interview, the technical team advices recruiter to look for next set of available candidates. Candidates who clear the initial level of technical interviews are moved for the next level of interview. The second level interviews may or may not be a client interview. In some cases client gives authority to the offshore project team to hire suitable candidates.

Client interviews are mostly telephonic interviews. Recruiter should confirm twice with the candidate on his availability to take the client interview. If there is a change, client has to be intimated well in advance. If client changes the schedule, the same has to be intimated to the candidates without fail.

For some senior positions, there may be two offshore technical interviews and a client interview depending upon the requirement. Client shortlists the suitable candidate and advices offshore company to hire. A senior person from the hiring team or HR Manager does the HR Interview to see the attitude, commitment, interest of the candidate to stick with the company for long time.

HR Manager takes a decision based on the Joining date, Salary fitment and other expectations of the candidate. HR Manager has authority not to offer a candidate based on the following findings;

- Fake Profile.
- Poor Attitude.
- Not sure about what candidate says (Honesty).
- High Salary Expectation.
- Joining Duration, etc.

The details are intimated to the client and the interview process starts from the beginning. If the candidate clears the HR interview, the positions are mentioned as closed. Likewise a candidate too has his own expectation with the company and he/she takes their own decision to accept or reject the offer. If the candidate rejects the offer, again the interview process starts and if he/she accepts the offer then the positions are mentioned as closed.

The offer, acceptance and the joining details of the candidate has to be well informed to the client so that they can schedule the job assignment to the candidate. Recruiter hand holds the candidate till joining and on-boarding them into the project. Only then the real open positions are closed. Most happening scenario in the market is that the candidate gets offer from couple or more companies to raise their compensation. Recruiter gets the information only at the last minute that the candidate is not joining and has taken another offer.

This is too late period for the recruiter to work on the back-up when a candidate does not join the company at the last minute. The time taken from sourcing to offering may be around 20 days approximately and if the candidate has two months of notice period to join, then ultimately recruiter waits for 80 days to fill a position. The effort of the recruiter, interviewer and the client goes in vain. So with the approval of the management, recruiter has to have a back-up for every offer they release.

Once after offering, there needs to be a regular conversation with the candidate and the recruiter needs to find the pulse of the candidate whether he/she will join the company. Recruiter needs to be open with the candidate on what will be the company situation if he/she doesn't join. If needed, recruiter should meet the candidate for a coffee and explain the positives of the company / project / team / growth etc.

Recruiter's real success will be making the offered candidate joining the company.

----xxxx-----

*For* **RECRUITMENT AGENCY ENVIRONMENT:**

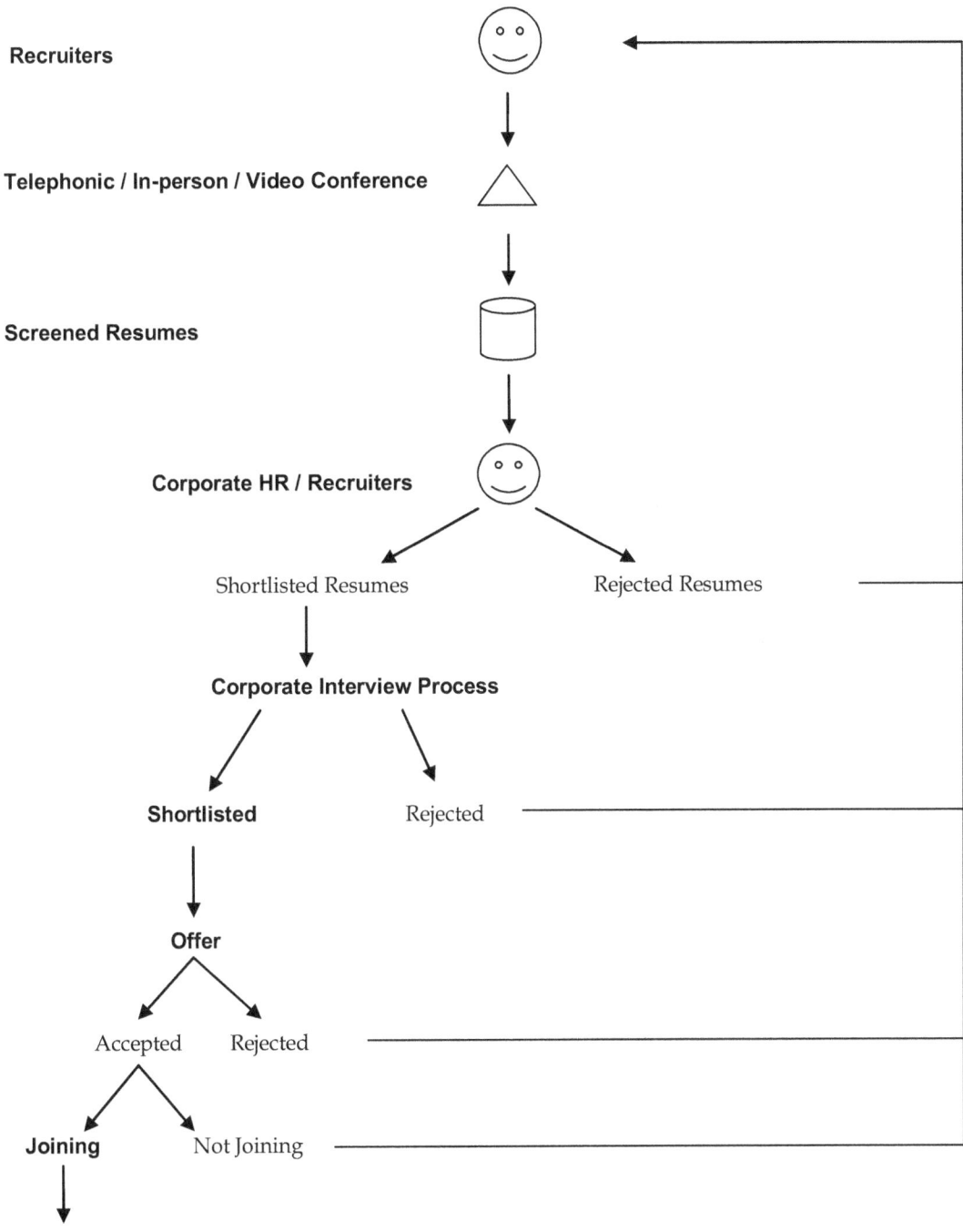

Recruiters

Telephonic / In-person / Video Conference

Screened Resumes

Corporate HR / Recruiters

Shortlisted Resumes                    Rejected Resumes

Corporate Interview Process

Shortlisted                    Rejected

Offer

Accepted        Rejected

Joining        Not Joining

On-Boarding into the Project

## *Process Description:*

The efforts of the recruiters are high in the placement agency compared to the efforts of recruiters in corporate and the same sourcing methods are followed. Recruiters in corporate environment work for their internal open positions alone. But the recruiters in placement agency work for multiple open positions / clients. A good recruiter has to be familiar in all the skills and can work for multiple open positions on a day.

Recruiters in placement agency sources resumes through various channels discussed before and the validation is done either through telephonic, video conference or in-person discussion. The suitable resumes are passed on to the corporate recruiters. Recruiters in the corporate know their client expectation and source the profiles accordingly. Since the recruiters in the placement agency are not directly interacting with the end clients, they may not know the expectations of the client. Recruiters in corporate has to explain clearly on the client needs and the profile expectation.

If the resume is not suitable, then there needs to be a note to the placement agency on what to look in the resume. If the resumes are suitable then the corporate interview method follows. When the resumes are sourced by the placement agency, they are responsible for candidates to take client interviews without fail. In this process recruiter in the placement agency acts only in resumes sourcing and interaction. They are not exposed to any corporate interview process. But otherwise the process of interacting with the candidate and on holding them till joining are same as discussed before.

# CABIN 10 – SELECTION METHODS

*FOR **FRESHERS:***

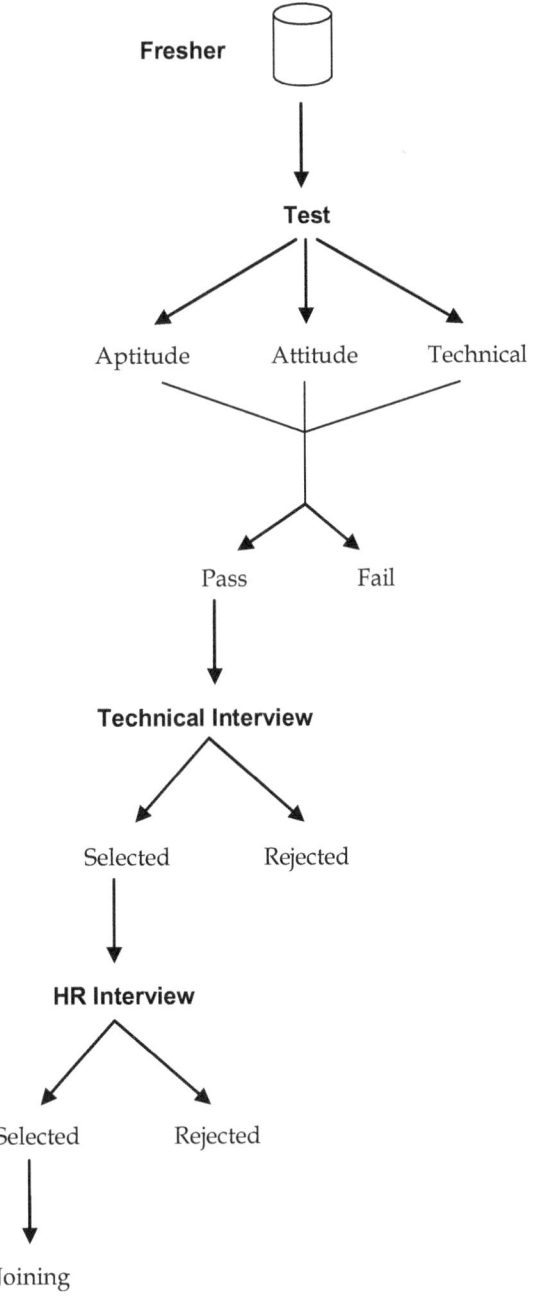

*Description:*

Hiring fresher is not as difficult as experienced candidates. The amount of candidates available in the market is high and the demand to offer them is very low. Recruiters have many options to hire a fresher. Even if they get rejected in Test or Interview process, it will not create huge impact on the hiring process.

The selection process for a fresher consists of the following;

- Aptitude, Attitude, Technical test
- Technical Interview with the offshore technical panel.
- HR Interviews, Offer and Joining.

The test can be combination of one or all mentioned above based on the company's need. Candidates who clear the test alone are scheduled for an offshore technical interview. No telephonic interviews are entertained for the fresher and all are in-person interviews. Normally clients do not engage themselves in interviewing fresher and the offshore company takes the decision to hire or reject a fresher based on the need.

## Test Methods

*Attitude Test:*
Recruiter assesses the candidate's analytical thinking and personality by an Attitude Test. Even though all the candidates has required Education Background, Percentage, Skills etc., their approach towards a situation / question will be different. A question has four or more different answers and situation and by the way of answering, the recruiter can find the attitude of the candidate. As you know there are two types of attitude i.e. Positive and Negative. Candidates with positive attitude get selected in the test.

*Aptitude Test:*
Aptitude Test is designed to assess the logical reasoning and thinking performance of the candidate. It is also known as the Psychology test. It consists of Numerical Reasoning, Graphs and Tables Reasoning, Diagrammatic reasoning, logical reasoning, Verbal Reasoning, Logic Test, Computer Aptitude Test, Vocabulary Test, Team Work Test etc. Candidates with logical reasoning get selected in the test.

*Technical Test:*
The Technical Test assesses the technical ability of the candidate. The questions are framed on the skills required for the opening or in-line with the expertise of the candidate's skill. Candidates with good scores in the test get selected.

----XXXX-----

*FOR **EXPERIENCED:***

This process is not common in all the companies. In most of the case, experienced candidates do not show interest to take up a test. It may be a speed breaker for recruiters to complete the assignment on time. Some of the companies follow the process of selecting experienced candidates (between 1-4 years) by asking them to undergo one or more test mentioned before. The technical questions are in-depth on the subject and will not be as basic as a fresher test. This process cuts the technically poor candidates and avoids wasting time of the individual / technical panel. Recruiter and the Management have to mutually decide if this process will help them to complete the task or it will put down the interest of the candidate.

# CABIN 11 – OFFER PROCESS

Offer Process is part of the Interview Process. In HR interview the HR Manager understands the technical and personal capability of the candidate. HR Manager takes a decision based on the Joining date, Salary fitment and other expectations of the candidate. HR Manager has authority not to offer a candidate based on the following findings;

- Fake Profile.
- Poor Attitude.
- Bad Communication Skills.
- Not sure about what candidate says (Honesty).
- Future Goals.
- High Salary Expectation.
- Joining Duration, etc.

Candidates tend to open up more about his/her compensation benefits in the discussion. HR Manager Offers a candidate finding the candidates Academic Qualification and other Educational Credentials are true, Total Experience and relevant, current compensation and other monetary benefits etc. HR Manager also compares the internal employees experience and compensation so that the candidate falls under same experience and CTC to avoid problems with employees.

HR Manager extends the offer to the candidates who got selected & following are the details required to complete the Offer Process;

- Staff Requisition Form duly filled by the Offshore Manager / Functional Manager which is approved by the Management.

- Updated Resume of the candidate.

- Interview Assessment Form duly filled by the interview panel (both 1st and 2nd level) with HR interview feedback.

- Email acceptance from the client, if additional client interview happened.

- Feedback by the HR Manager to hire with proposed compensation and joining details.

On accepting the proposal from the HR Manager, candidate signs the offer letter which is duly signed by the signing authority of the company. On the committed date the candidate is expected to join the company.

If the proposal is not accepted by the candidate because of compensation issues, HR Manager sees the fitment of the company's compensation matrix to see if the offer can be revised. If it is not possible, HR Manager Advices the Recruitment team to look for alternative candidate for the position.

## No Show

*"No Show"* is the absence of the candidate either to take the interview or to join the offered company without prior notification. Most happening scenario in the market is that the candidate gets offer from couple or more companies to raise their compensation. Recruiter gets the information only at the last minute that the candidate is not joining and has taken another offer.

This is too late period for the recruiter to work on the back-up when a candidate does not join the company at the last minute. The time taken from sourcing to offering may be around 20 days approximately and if the candidate has two months of notice period to join, then ultimately recruiter waits for 80 days to fill a position. The effort of the recruiter, interviewer and the client goes in vain. So with the approval of the management, recruiter has to have a back-up for every offer they release.

Once after offering, there needs to be a regular conversation with the candidate and the recruiter needs to find the pulse of the candidate whether he/she will join the company. Recruiter needs to be open with the candidate on what will be the company situation if he/she doesn't join. If needed, recruiter should meet the candidate over a coffee and explain the positives of the company / project / team / growth etc.

Recruiter's real success will be making the offered candidate joining the company.

# CABIN 12 – JOINING / ON-BOARDING PROCESS

The Recruitment Life Cycle successfully ends by on-boarding suitable candidates for the open positions. The candidate interacts with the HR-Recruiter from the date of applying the job till joining. So, Recruiter is the right person to give a warm welcome to the new employee joining the company. As per company's policy, Recruiter confirms that the candidate has brought the needed documents to do the join formalities.

Basic documents needed for On-boarding the candidate;

- Copy of the signed offer letter (If sent through courier / post).
- Photocopies of the educational qualifications.
- Passport size photos (As per company's policy).
- Offer and Reliving letters of previous work experience (Not applicable for Fresher).
- Experience Certificates.
- Recent salary statements to verify the compensation.
- Address and age proof for identification.
- Passport copy (if applicable).
- Last financial year income tax submission form (Not applicable for Fresher).

With the above mentioned documents, the company joining documents need to be duly filled by the new joiner and the same to be submitted to the HR team. Recruiter introduces the candidate to his colleagues, senior management and the project members to make the On-boarding process smooth. Recruiter's job end here and the core HR team take care of the candidate for Induction and other employee engagement activities.

By On-Boarding the candidate, the Recruiter successfully completes the Recruitment Life Cycle.

# CABIN 13 – KRA OF A RECRUITER

Key Result Area of a Recruiter is the job responsibility allocated to a Recruiter in an organization. It is the outcome or the expectation of a recruiter to perform his/her tasks in a company. Yearly salary appraisal of a recruiter is closely connected to their KRA. Recruitment Manager finds the efforts of a recruiter taken to close open positions in a financial year. The KRA also helps to understand if the recruitment has been a profit centre for the company. Recruiter's KRA may differ from company's policies but, below given are some common job responsibilities of a Recruiter.

- Understand / evaluate the Job Requirements.
- To handle end-to-end Recruitment Process.
- Ability to interact (Communication skills).
- Sourcing Methods.
- Good Interviewing Skills.
- Hiring Domain Knowledge (Technical Expertise for IT / Telecom Recruiters)
- Knowledge and Experience to utilize Recruitment Tools.
- Good in Recruitment Cycle time (Closure time).
- Good in Reports Management.
- Background Verification.

## ABILITY TO UNDERSTAND AND EVALUATE THE JOB REQUIREMENTS

Recruiter needs to understand the requirement with his past experience. If you are a fresher in Recruitment, the Hiring Manager will help you to understand the expectations of the client. It is advisable to go through the job description first and discuss with your colleagues and seniors that you have understood the requirement. Incase if the requirement is not clear, Recruiter must discuss with the client or concern offshore manager before moving into next step.

## ABILITY TO HANDLE END-TO-END RECRUITMENT PROCESS

Recruiter to be familiar on the recruitment process from the job initiation to on-boarding the candidate discussed in previous chapters. Understanding of the recruitment life cycle is very important as it forms the base for all the other recruitment process. To complete the KRA set by the Recruitment Manager / Management, Recruiter should be able to handle end to end Recruitment Process.

# ABILITY TO INTERACT

Proper communication helps recruiters to make an impression among others. Particularly, it is a must skill when interacting with Clients and Candidates for a discussion, clarifications, interview scheduling, offer process etc. Poor communication not only puts recruiter in a bad situation, but also the reputation of the company comes down. Recruiters with good communication can put things on right track and complete the interview process in a smooth manner.

### *Ability to coordinate*

Recruiters need to make a bond with the hiring managers and the candidates. So that recruiter can get enough support from the hiring managers to understand the resource / skills expectation and Candidates for Profile needs, Interview schedule, Offering and Joining. Particularly, recruiters in placement agency has to communicate well with their clients in order to get new requirements, make presentations about their agency, understanding client expectation, profile follow-up, interview schedule, offer process and candidates follow through.

# PROFILE SOURCING THROUGH COST EFFECTIVE CHANNELS

Before getting into action, Recruiter must know the Recruitment Budget allocated by the management for a job opening. By which, Recruiter should take necessary action to hire by self or to tie up with the placement agency or any other recruitment sources. Recruiter's KRA will also be to cut down the recruitment cost of the company as it will also be reflected in the Recruiter's appraisal.

# HIRING DOMAIN KNOWLEDGE

To find if the resume matches the job responsibility, recruiter must possess domain knowledge on what skills / technologies they are hiring. Only when a recruiter is strong in the hiring domain, he/she can find suitable profiles for the job opening. For a fresh recruiter, he/she can get the help of seniors to explain them about the needed resource. Experienced recruiters who are good in some regular technical hiring but now he/she has given new skills to hire, then their need a knowledge up-gradation by finding the skill terminology online , through references, books etc. Best way to understand the Domain / Skills by discussing with the internal project managers or the client.

# GOOD IN RESUME AND CANDIDATE EVALUATION SKILLS (PRELIMINARY INTERVIEWS)

Recruiter filters / evaluates the candidates by meeting them in person or preliminary HR interview over phone to over phone to understand the candidate's suitability for the open position. The screening methods are given in Cabin -7 by which a resume can be screened for client /offshore manager's review.

### *Duplicate Resume*

 A Duplicate Resume refers to the profile which has been applied already and viewed / called / scheduled interview by the recruiter for a job opening.  It is always an additional work and time consuming job for the recruiter to find if the resume is already in his/her database. For example, the job opening is floated to multiple placement agencies and if same resume is sent by two or more placement agencies, the resume is considered as a Duplicate Resume. The credit should be given to the recruiter, who sourced the resume, spoken to the candidates and sent first to the corporate recruiter.

If the corporate recruiter sources the resume first, then the recruiter has authority to reject the resumes sent by the placement agencies. Recruiter identifies the duplicate resume using Manual and Automated process. Manual spreadsheet contains name of the candidate, years of experience, location, skills, years of experience, relevant experience, applied date, interviewed for the project etc. Automated process detects and identifies the duplicate resume with the information stored by the recruiter in the software before. It gives the recruiter to discard the resume saved in the software or updates the old resume or delete the resume from the software so that confusions on the current credentials of the candidate can be avoided.

It is important to avoid sending same resumes to the hiring manager / client for the same position. It will create a bad impression on the recruiter.

## EFFECTIVE UTILIZATION OF RECRUITMENT TOOLS

Recruiters need to use the given recruitment tools effectively to complete the allocated recruitment task. Also the recruiter should understand when to use what tools such as Job boards, Placement Agency, Head hunting, Social Networking sites, Advertisements etc. Depending upon the skills, years of experience and the niche demands of the job, recruiter should cleverly take decisions on the sourcing channels. It is important to reduce the cost of hiring but at the same time recruiter should also understand the criticality of the project. If the open positions need to be closes on the specific time and if it takes some hiring costs, recruiters should discuss with their Recruitment Manager / Management on the hiring needs.

## QUICK TURNAROUND TIME

Once the Job is initiated, recruiters need to respond the offshore manager / client with the first set of resumes. Recruiter need to respond with the first set of resumes in 24 hours of time or earlier as it will create a good impression with the Hiring Manager. It is important to respond immediately for emails and calls sent by the Management, Client and the Candidates for resume submission, interview co-ordination, Interview schedule, Offer Process and Joining intimation etc.,

### Qualitative Resumes
Quick turnaround doesn't mean that recruiters can send any kind of resumes to the hiring manager / client. Profiles which suits the job requirement alone need to sent. Corporate Recruiter circulates the job opening to many placement agencies. Recruiters in placement agency need to send qualitative resumes to the client for long term work relationship.

### Hit Ratio to be increased
The Hit Ratio or the Conversion Ratio is very important as it may prolong or shorten the Recruitment Cycle Time. The example is given in the Recruitment Cycle Time of a Recruiter in Cabin – 4. Recruiter is expected to close the open positions as soon as possible since it is connected to the billing of the hiring resource for the company.

## REPORTS MANAGEMENT

Based on the company's recruitment policy, Recruiter has to update Management on his/her hiring activities with Daily, Weekly and Monthly Recruitment Reports. The reports can be either Manual or Software driven to provide a precise details to the management.

**In a placement agency**, it is mandatory to submit Daily Report is must. The recruiter's day to day efforts are tracked by the seniors / management in order to find if their efforts are in the right direction. End of every day, recruiter should submit the report to his/her seniors and it should contain the following details;

    a.  Date.

    b.  Name of the candidate.

    c.  Experience (Total & Relevant).

    d.  Skills.

    e.  Current Company.

    f.  Current CTC.

    g.  Expected CTC.

    h.  Joining Time if offered.

    i.  Name of the client.

Depends upon recruiters interest and agency need, the spreadsheet can also contain the following to follow-up with the client;

    j.  Resume sent to client on (Date) – Feedback received on (Date)

    k.  Profile status (Shortlisted / Rejected).

    l.  Interview date.

    m.  Interview Status (Selected / Rejected).

    n.  Offered date - Joining.

    o.  Candidate's status (Joined / No Show).

The Weekly Report touches the overall efforts of a recruiter for a particular week. This report is generated to check the overall status of a recruiter and the efforts are discussed in a weekly meeting organized by the seniors. Recruiters need to give a justification on their performance and what went right / wrong in the week. The weekly report varies from agency to agency depending on their need but the below given details are mandatory;

    a.  Weekly Report date.

    b.  No of profiles sourced by the recruiter.

    c.  No of profiles sent to each client.

    d.  Details of profiles awaiting client feedback.

e.  No of profiles shortlisted.

f.  No of profiles interviewed.

g.  No of candidates shortlisted.

h.  No of candidates offered.

i.  Details of candidates joined / No show.

The Monthly Report touches brief notes of the recruiter's efforts and this will be useful in case the placement agency management decides to motivate the recruiter in the form of incentives, bonus, gifts, tours or any motivational ideas. In the monthly recruitment team meeting, each recruiter should address his/her seniors with a data containing following details;

a.  No of assignment worked in a month.

b.  No of profiles sourced.

c.  No of Shortlisted candidates / Selection Ratio.

d.  Joined / No Show.

e.  No of positions open.

Recruiters need to give justification on what methods worked or what went wrong during the month. This kind of daily, weekly, monthly reports not only updates the management on the recruiter's efforts. But also it is a self learning process for the recruiter to understand where he/she needs improvements while hiring.

**In a Corporate**, the reports may vary from company to company. The Daily / Weekly / Monthly reports contain same details as followed by the recruiter in the recruitment agency. Here the corporate recruiter sends resume to the internal hiring manager or a client. The reports are verified by the Recruitment Manager or by the Management in order to find the efforts of the Recruiter.

## BACKGROUND VERIFICATION OF THE SELECTED CANDIDATE

Background Verifications are of two types; One, Pre Employment and Secondly, Post Employment. Recruiter's job is to do Pre Employment verification and help the HR colleagues with Post Employment verification. Every company needs a clean candidate with good Educational qualifications, Work experience, and Technical skills etc. Every company's employees bring valuable client relationship, revenue, image etc, from their clients. So having employees with a clean and clear background is a must.
In reality, an average of 35% of the candidates tend to goof-up their Educational details, Work experience, Salary details, any Criminal Records Skill details etc. Important for recruiters to hire an ethical candidate either by themselves or through a verification agency to find the details mentioned in the resume are true.

Post Employment Verifications are mostly done by the external verification agency as the HR/Recruiter lacks time for investigation. Following are the checks done and the reports are submitted to the HR for perusal;

a. Education

b. Resume Validation

c. Employment

d. Site Visit

e. Address verification

f. Identity check

g. PAN Card/Drivers License/Passport verification (In US: SSN check)

h. Criminal Records, Regulatory and Compliance Databases Search

i. Drug Testing

j. Nationality check

k. Marital status check

l. Date of Birth check

m. Reference Check

# CABIN 14 - PRACTICAL HIRING

Till now we were discussing on the theoretical portions of Hiring. Theoretical knowledge helps recruiters to form a base for their recruitment career. To become a successful Recruiter one has to convert his/her theoretical knowledge into practical experience by taking decisions upon situational demands. Whether the recruiter is in a corporate environment or in a placement agency, the hiring process is same. Based on the company's goal, project / client expectation, candidate's availability, recruiter can change gears to close the open positions. Strong theoretical knowledge on hiring gives confidence, better approach and improve decision making skills.

The above mentioned chapters are mandatory basic process in the recruitment industry. The reporting structure, hiring plans, policies, requirement details, hiring manager and their relationship differs from company to company. For example, in the Recruitment Life Cycle we have shown as Offshore Manager or a Sales Manager initiates the Job requirement. The process will be same but instead of a Sales Manager, Client can directly send the job specifications to the Company Management or the local Project Manager. Person and their designation may vary, but process is same. Likewise, recruiters in the placement agency can get requirements directly from the Recruitment Manager of a Corporate or it can come through the Placement Agency Manager / Team Leaders but process is same.

Before sending resumes to the Hiring Manager, Recruiter should discuss in detail about the job opening with the candidates. If the candidates are not aware of the complete job opening, they may skip interviews and that will create a bad impression on the recruiter. Be open on the CTC and joining dates of the candidate. Let the management know what you have found in the market on candidates availability. Do not hide candidate's negative stuffs with the client / hiring manager. Always maintain a good rapport with the internal employees; this will get good profile reference when ever needed.

Recruiter needs to apply correct key words in the job portal to get the suitable profiles. Recruiter should know when to apply a Boolean search, Magic search and a Basic search. The job portal contains millions of profiles and it is designed such a way that only certain number of profiles can be viewed per day / week / month according to our purchase. On a first search, if Recruiter gets only an X quantity of profiles, then he/she should not decide that there are only few applicants matching to their opening. When you do a same search after couple of days, you can see some older dated resume available in the portal. The mistake is not with the recruiter, it is a business trick performed by the job portals to keep you in their client list for long time.

There is a possibility that the candidates who have applied in the job portal a year ago may look for a change now. It will be wise for a recruiter not only to check the latest active profiles but also to mine the older resumes to find the interest. It may or may not give result, but trying something new makes any harm and is better than doing nothing. While sending the resumes to the client or the hiring manager, always mark a copy to the Recruitment Manager or your immediate senior. If you don't get feedback for your resumes, ask gently or give a reminder to the hiring team. Secondly, escalate it to your seniors. If you don't update the day to day happenings to your seniors, then you will be taking for ride.

# EXIT AREA

## ABOUT AUTHOR

**Vijay Anand L.V** has an overall 10 years of experience in the Recruitment Industry. Currently holds a Bachelor of Science from Madras University, Chennai, and Master of Labour Management from Madurai Kamaraj University, Madurai and a Post Graduate degree in Human Resources Management, Pondicherry. Working experience includes Leading Consultancy Services and IT/Telecom software companies in Chennai, India.

**Twitter id** – vanandhr
**Gmail and Facebook email id** – vanandhr@gmail.com

## DISCLAIMER

This book "Hiring Handbook" is written using my own industry experience and recruitment knowledge. It has not been copied from any other text books or videos or contents and has not used other's copy rights.

www.ingramcontent.com/pod-product-compliance
Lightning Source LLC
Chambersburg PA
CBHW081227170526
45165CB00009B/2987